Isaiah 26:3-4
"PERFECT PEACE XI"
Door

VANESSA RAYNER

authorHOUSE®

AuthorHouse™
1663 Liberty Drive
Bloomington, IN 47403
www.authorhouse.com
Phone: 1 (800) 839-8640

Published by AuthorHouse 02/10/2016

ISBN: 978-1-5246-7084-9 (sc)
ISBN: 978-1-5246-7083-2 (e)

Print information available on the last page.

This book is printed on acid-free paper.

A GIFT . . .

*P*resented to

_____

*F*rom

_____

*D*ate

_____

I DON'T UNDERSTAND
EVERYTHING GOD DOES;
BUT I TRUST HIM IN
EVERYTHING. . . HALLELUJAH!

TABLE OF CONTENTS

Theme

The message of **Isaiah 26:3-4** is concerning *"Perfect Peace."* This is the distinct and unifying composition of this book with the subtitle <u>Door</u>.

<u>The King James Version</u>

3. Thou wilt keep him in perfect peace,
whose mind is stayed on thee:
because
he trusteth in thee.
4. Trust ye in the LORD for ever:
for in the LORD JEHOVAH
is everlasting strength:

PRAYER

Oh Heavenly Father,
I pray that this book will bless everyone that reads it.
I pray that it will inspire your people to strive to keep
their minds, hearts, souls and spirits
on YOU, more . . . . each day!

I pray that saints are learning to
experience Your "Perfect Peace"
in a new and exciting way, every day,
all day and throughout the day.

Father God, I ask in Jesus' name that
the Holy Spirit will bring
this knowledge back to their
remembrance as Your people
walk through doors, see doors, or hear the word door.

Lord, I'm grateful for the assignment, You
given me in Your kingdom work.
I thank You for blessing those that help
make Your work able to go forth.

Father in the Gospel of Matthew and Mark,
You made it clear that You will reward
those that bless your servant.
It could be by prayer, words of
encouragement, to even given
that person a cup of water.

**And if you give even a cup of cold water
to one of the least of my followers,
you will surely be rewarded.**
Matthew 10:42 NLT

Father God,
I give you all the Glory, Honor and
Praise in Jesus' name. Amen.

AUTHOR'S NOTES

Author notes normally provide a way to add extra information to one's book that may be awkward and inappropriate to include in the text of the book itself. It provides supplemental contextual details on the aspects of the book. It can help readers understand the book content and the background details of the book better. ***The times and dates of researching, reading, and gathering this information are not included; mostly when I typed on it.

***Will elaborate on this statement in back of book in a new section, just drop in my spirit at 0613 on January 14, 2017, titled A Reader's Question.

1049; Sunday, 10 April 2016; Just added a phrase taken from "Perfect Peace X" Dreams for this book "A Gift . . ." page. A few minutes ago, I sent in the corrections for "Perfect Peace X" book. Not sure what this book will be about or titled, at the moment. I going to make me a smoothie shake, and ride down to Arkabutla Lake in MS for a little RR.

2145; Friday, 15 April 2016; By the way, Arkabutla Lake was closed because of flooding. Just added the date in which "Perfect Peace X" was published to the page titled Other Books by the Author. I'm still not sure what this book will be about. I'm just moving in faith.

1947; Sunday, 30 October 2016; Glory Be to God! This book will be titled <u>Door</u>. I was at Target this evening around 1725, and I was looking at a puzzle box which had nothing but doors on it. It caught my attention to the point that I was staring at the various doors on the box, the word "the door" dropped in my spirit; I just smile. I had been asking Father God was writing books over in my life for over three months. Well, I assume not. Let me get busy researching. Happy Birthday Henry Lee, you are greatly missed.

1641; Wednesday, 02 November 2016

1725; Friday, 04 November 2016

1929; Monday, 07 November 2016

1746; Thursday, 10 November 2016

0931; Friday, 11 November 2016; Happy Veteran Day! Everyone . . .

Family who served ~

Ambous Lee Moore -Dad

AD Moore -Brother

Alvin L. Jackson -Son

Dalvin Moore -Nephew

Charles A. Jones Jr. -Son

Regina C. Moore -Sister

Dadrien Moore -Nephew

1955; Sunday, 13 November 2016; Went to Bellevue Baptist Church 6pm service for the 2nd time. A perfect stranger named Ms. Carol Brame asked could she sit next to me, to pray with me. She also gave me her phone number and invited me to

Sunday School Class on Sundays at 11 am, Room 156. It really blessed my soul, more than she will ever know. Hallelujah!

1955; Monday, 14 November 2016

2022; Tuesday, 15 November 2016

1830; Wednesday, 16 November 2016

1719; Monday, 21 November 2016

1800; Tuesday, 22 November 2016

1731; Wednesday, 23 November 2016

0626; Sunday, 04 December 2016

2008; Tuesday, 06 December 2016

1810; Wednesday, 07 December 2016

1548; Thursday, 08 December 2016

0723; Sunday, 11 December 2016

1334; Tuesday, 13 December 2016; AW interview ~ I put it all in your hands, Father God!

1709; Wednesday, 14 December 2016; Wasn't awarded the AW position, however, my 1st Christmas Gift (Royal Mix Toasted and Salted Nuts from Sunnylandfarms) was on the front porch sent by my oldest sister, Easter Mae from Arkansas. Hallelujah is the highest praise!

1721; Friday, 16 December 2016; It's cold today.

0539; Saturday, 17 December 2016

1024; Sunday, 18 December 2016

1934; Tuesday, 20 December 2016; Watching Grizzles game on Television, up by 7 points....end of the 1st quarter.

0738; Monday, 26 December 2016

0942; Tuesday, 27 December 2016

1723; Wednesday, 28 December 2016

1620; Friday, 30 December 2016

1123; Saturday, 31 December 2016; Reading Over Text, Filling In Details and Proofreading Begins

0851; Sunday, 01 January 2017; Song and Praised the New Year in with family at Lincoln Church of Christ in Alamo, Tn where Yogi Woods is the Pastor. I had a glorious time!

0826; Monday, 02 January 2017

0136; Tuesday, 03 January 2017

1229; Wednesday, 04 January 2017;Just made it home from the dentist's office.

1656; Thursday, 05 January 2017

1648; Friday, 06 January 2017

0011; Saturday, 07 January 2017

0936; Saturday, 07 January 2017; Back at it.

0100; Sunday, 08 January 2017

1815; Sunday, 08 January 2017; Back at it.

1744; Monday, 09 January 2017

1747; Tuesday, 10 January 2017;took 3 hours of comp time, left work at 1:00pm got my hair fix, hands and feet done. Just made it home & ready to go to bed. I'm going to try stay up an hour or so . . .

2050; Wednesday, 11 January 2017

1639; Thursday, 12 January 2017

1631; Friday, 13 January 2017

0558; Saturday, 14 January 2017

1751; Sunday, 15 January 2017

0109; Monday, 16 January 2017

1747; Monday, 16 January 2017; Back at it, on Martin Luther King Jr. Day. Earlier today Prophet Daniel Morris and I went to visit Apostle Dorothy Smith in Sikeston, Mo. We ate at Lambert Restaurant, prayed at her home, and had a glorious time before we left.

1827; Tuesday, 17 January 2017

1734; Wednesday, 18 January 2017

1644; Thursday, 19 January 2017

1634; Friday, 20 January 2017

0605; Tuesday, 31 January 2017; A quick look over before emailing it to AuthorHouse.

PREFACE

Isaiah 26:3-4, "Perfect Peace XI" ~ <u>Door</u>

The book <u>Isaiah 26:3-4, "Perfect Peace XI" Door</u> is the 11th book in a series called Isaiah 26:3-4, "Perfect Peace." LORD, I bless Your Holy Name, the King of Kings, our Bright Morning Star, and our Prince of Peace. Hallelujah!

It all started from how I drew near to the LORD in my workplace by keeping my mind on Him. I related numbers, you see throughout the day, everywhere, on almost everything on Him, His word, biblical events and facts to give me peace in the midst of chaos.

It's our desire for you to discover the power of the Holy Spirit by numbers, words, places, people, and things related to doors. **Remember**, the LORD Jesus <u>PROMISED us tribulation</u> while we were in this world.

> ***These things, I have spoken unto you,***
> ***that in me ye might have peace.***
> ***In the world ye shall have tribulation:***
> ***But be of good cheer;***
> ***I have overcome the world.***
> John 16:33 KJV

However, we have been <u>PROMISED His peace</u> while we endure these trials, tribulations, troubles, and tests. Perfect Peace is given only to those whose mind and heart reclines upon the LORD. God's peace is increased in us according to the knowledge of His Holy Word.

> ***Grace and peace be multiplied unto you***
> ***through the knowledge of God,***
> ***and of Jesus our LORD.***
> *2* Peter 1:2 KJV

It's our hope that <u>Isaiah 26:3-4, "Perfect Peace XI" Door</u> will forever bring joy and peace to your heart; when you enters a door(s) or see a door(s), this day forward. May the peace of God rule, rest and abide, forever.

THANKS   *To the Readers . . .*

As a disciple of the LORD Jesus Christ, I have learned true success and happiness come when we are seeking and striving to do God's purpose for our lives. True success lies in doing God's will; not in fame and fortune.

On behalf of our Heavenly Father Ministry, I want to thank you for your support.

Thanks for helping me spread "Perfect Peace" through your e-mail, Facebook, Twitter, LinkedIn, Instagram, Tumblr, and etc. accounts to your family, friends, neighbors, co-workers, church family, internet social friends and associates.

Remember, you may not know until you get to heaven just how much a song you sung, kind words spoken by you or even a book you suggested reading, at the right moment, encourage a person to keep on going when a few minutes before they were tempted to give up on life and their walk with the LORD.

I greatly appreciate your love and kindness to this ministry.

So, my dear brothers and sisters, be strong and immovable. Always work enthusiastically for the Lord, for you know that nothing you do for the Lord is ever useless. 1 Corinthians 15:58 NLT

Acknowledgements

I wish to express my sincere gratitude to a perfect stranger; Ms. Carol Brame that asked could she sit next to me, to pray with me at Bellevue Baptist Church in Memphis, Tn. on November 13, 2016, at the Sunday 6:00 pm evening service.

I needed that prayer and was truly blessed more than she will ever know. The words, in that prayer she prayed to me, were inspiring as well as deep. It swells my soul with praise. It encouraged my mind in understanding and warmed my heart in giving God thanks, regardless of my present confusing, and unpleasant circumstance I was in. Hallelujah!!

Confession: Sorry to say, as of today (12/31/2016), I haven't made it to the Sunday School Class she invited me to. She also gave me her phone number which I haven't used. Father God, please forgive me for my slothfulness.

Attending Sunday School Class at Bellevue Baptist Church is definite one of my New Year Resolution, Father God.

INTRODUCTION

*For Those Who Want To Be
Kept In "Perfect Peace"*

This book was prepared and written to open your mind to a "Perfect Peace" that comes only from God. I'm striving to elevate you into a "Unique and Profound" awareness of God's presence around you at all time.

According to some people, it's hard to keep your mind on the LORD. While most Christians will agree that if you keep your mind stayed on the LORD, He will keep you in "Perfect Peace." This is why so many people enjoy going to church on Sundays and attending midweek services for peace and joy that they receive, but only for a short time.

You can experience the peace of the LORD throughout the day and every day. His unspeakable joy, his strength, his "Perfect Peace" in the midst of the storm whether it's at work, home, college, school, etc. You can also experience this peace, even when your day is going well.

This concept of this book was placed in my spirit by our Father, which art in heaven, to help me when he allowed Satan to test me at my workplace until he finished molding me into a MAP; (Minister/Ambassador/Pastor).

Throughout these pages, I will be focussing on biblical events, and facts surrounding the word "Door." However, I am sure much more can be said on this word, so these examples serve merely as an introduction and are not exhaustive by any means.

DEDICATION

To Target,
601 Colonial Rd., Memphis, Tn. 38117,
where I received my revelation & inspiration for this book,
in the toy department.

CHAPTER 1

Revelation 3:20

The first chapter of this book begins with one of my favorite Bible verses. It's also the first verse, I learnt-by-heart with the word "door" in it. First of all, it's in the New Testament, it's the 27ᵗʰ book in the New Testament with 21 chapters; The Book of Revelation. This book has been called the Revelation to John, the Apocalypse of John, The Revelation, Revelation and Apocalypse by scholars. It was written by the Apostle John at Patmos. John had been exiled to the prison island because he wouldn't stop preaching the Gospel of Jesus Christ. While he was there, John was visited by the Lord. He commanded him to write the visions He revealed to him on a tablet.

Behold,
I stand at the door, and knock:
if any man hear my voice, and open the door,
I will come in to him, and will sup
with him, and he with me.
Revelation 3:20 KJV

This verse begins with **"Behold"** in the King James Version. The word "Behold" means to fix the eyes upon, to see with attention, to observe fully with care. In the NIV Bible, it reads, "Here I am!" While other versions of the Bible, it says, Listen, Look, Now pay attention, Look at me,

See, Take note, Hinei, and Lo. It's a call to make sure we are seeing and hearing clearly and accurately. The word "Behold" is mentioned 1298 times in the King James Version.

The word "Behold" is mentioned first in the book of Genesis. God spoke this to Adam and Eve, whom he had made in his image and likeness. He gave them dominion over the earth and sea, and all things in them.

And God said,
Behold,
I have given you every herb bearing seed,
which is upon the face of all the earth,
and every tree, in the which is the
fruit of a tree yielding seed;
to you it shall be for meat.
Genesis 1:29 KJV

The next few words in my favorite verse read, **"I stand at the door, and knock."** These gracious words declare that Christ is at the door of a sinner's heart, waiting patiently for his/her to open the door of their hearts to accept Him.

A painting of Jesus knocking at a door was inspired by an English Pre-Raphaelite artist named William Holman Hunt born in 1827. In the painting, Jesus is preparing to knock on an unopened door. Note, the door in the picture has no outside handle, and can only be opened from the inside. In Jesus day, and most Middle Eastern cultures, knocking at a door was considered a form of importunity.

Note of Interest: The major Middle Eastern religious culture groups were Judaism, Christianity, and Islam. Some of the smaller religious groups were Gnosticism, Samaritanism, Druze, Mandaeism, Yarsanism, Shabakism, Ishikism, Zoroastrianism, etc.

~~~

The next few words, **"if any man hears my voice, and open the door,"** initially made reference to the members of the church in Laodicea. However, it would benefit every human being to hear the Saviour's voice and open the door so he can come into your life. He does not force the door open; He only enters if it is voluntarily opened.

Note of Interest: The city was originally named Diospolis, "the city of Jupiter" and then Rhoas. It was given the name Laodicea by King Antiochus II, after his wife. It was rebuilt and populated with Syrians and Jews who migrated from Babylonia, located 10 miles from Colossae, 48 miles from Philadelphia and 96 miles from Ephesus. Laodicea was one of Asia Minor's most flourishing cities built on seven hills. The sheep was known as fine black wool, and the city also minted coinage. It was destroyed by an earthquake during the 10th reign of Emperor Nero, around AD 64, along with Colossae, and Hierapolis.

~~~

The verse ends with these words, "**I will come in to him, and will sup with him, and he with me.** This is an image denoting acceptance, fellowship, intimacy and friendship. In ancient times to eat together, to break bread together has been the symbol of friendship, and this is what the Saviour promise here. Christ's offer to dine with the repentant church speaks of communion and intimacy. The word "dine" come from "deipneo" which refers to the last meal of the day; the evening meal. The underlying Greek meaning is rendered "sup," "supper," and "supped."

This verse was spoken to the church of Laodicea. It was the last and worst of the seven churches of Asia. Laodicea was a lukewarm church. They were neither cold nor were they hot for the Lord. The Lord said in verse 16, "because thou art lukewarm, nor neither cold nor hot, I will spew thee out of my mouth" meaning He will not own and acknowledge Laodicea as His; but cast her out.

What are the names of the other six churches? Smile . . .

1._____

2._____

3._____

4._____

5._____

6._____

7. Laodicea

You can do it . . . pray and think
Answer in back of book

CHAPTER 2

The Word "Door"

The origin of the word "door" comes from Middle English. Middle English is the language that was spoken and written in England between c.1150 to c.1500. The word "door" mergers from the Old English word "*dor*" and "*duru.*"

A door is typically used as an opening or closing to an entranceway. It could be part of a cabinet, a piece of furniture, placed on appliances or installed on vehicles. A door can be made from a solid piece of wood, aluminum, glass, fiberglass, composite, vinyl or metal. Some doors are designed to open and close on hinges while other doors swings or slides open and close.

There are many types of doors. The front door is considered the most popular door because every house, business, church, banks, organization or any establishment has one. Front doors come in many assorted colors. The constructions of these doors can range from all-steel to fiberglass with unique finishes. Other door finishes are wax, oil, green wood, varnish, stain, dye, and wood preserver.

The majority of houses also have interior doors that are used at the doorway of bathrooms, bedrooms, closets and some hallways. There are the beautiful and energy-efficient exterior doors such as the back door, storm door, and patio door. The patio door is either a sliding door or hinged doors with 2 or 3 door arrangements.

Note of Interests: In 3000 B.C., Ancient Egyptians built the first flat-top house of sun-dried bricks. In 2500 B.C., the Assyrians adopted this method of building but discovered that putting bricks in a fire made them harder and stronger. The Ancient Greeks built stone houses with slanted roofs. They were the first to put doors in their homes. Heron of Alexandria invented the first automatic door, in the 1st century A.D. The first automatic door used heat from a fire lit by the city's temple priest to open and close.

~~~

There are many other types and styles of doors. A half-door is also called a stable door which is divided in half horizontally. The top half of this door can be opened to feed animals, while the bottom half remains closed to keep the animal inside. Saloon doors, sometimes called café doors are a pair of lightweight swing doors often found in public bars. French doors consist of a frame around one or more transparent panels that may be installed individually, in a series or as matching pairs. A louvered door has fixed or movable wooden fins which permits open ventilation, while preserving privacy.

There are composite doors that have a single leaf door that can be solid or with glass. There are steel security doors which are made from sturdy steel, often for use in vaults and safe rooms. A bi-fold door is a unit that has several sections, folding in pairs. A sliding glass door sometimes called an Arcadia door, or patio door is made of glass which slides open and sometimes has a screen.

These types of doors are made from several types of materials which could be wood, steel, glass, aluminum, fiberglass, etc. Doors also are made in various shape and sizes to serve different purposes. However, a standard US residential exterior door sizes are 36" x 80". The residential interior doors are often smaller about 30" X 80."

There's a movie titled "Doors," and it's about <u>Doors</u>, a 1960-1970 American rock band which emphasizes the life of the lead singer, Jim Morrison. Another movie with the word "door" is "Sliding Doors," and it's a 1998 romantic comedy. Some doors in movies/shows/sitcoms will always be remembered.

1. <u>Star Trek,</u> The Forbidden Planet has one of the best and most elaborate heavy-duty doors in sci-fi. It's a semi-hexagon and opens in three one-foot-thick layers in different directions.
2. <u>Gone with the Wind</u>, in the final scene of this movie, Rhett Butler is seeing leaving Scarlett O'Hara through the front door of Tara. This symbolizes Rhett finally drawing an end to the poisonous relationship he's found himself in.
3. <u>The Wizard of Oz</u>, the door to Emerald City.
4. <u>The Exorcist,</u> one of cinema's most active doors, frequently opening and closing itself during the harrowing scene of Reagan's exorcism.

5. <u>Friends</u>, Monica's apartment door is a purple apartment door with a small yellow picture frame on the back of the door.

6. <u>The Hobbit/Lord of the Rings,</u> Bag End's front door is a tiny, round, green door and was the entrance to Biblo Baggains' home.

There are well-known historical doors that are precious, and some of them are mentioned in the next Chapter. The old ancient Bible doors were made from timber. The doors of King Solomon's temple were made from olive wood, carved with cherubim, flowers, palm trees and overlaid with gold, 1 Kings 6:31-35.

These doors were decorated with
carvings of cherubim,
palm trees, and open flowers
– all overlaid evenly with gold.
1 Kings 6:35 NLT

CHAPTER 3

Well-Known Doors

There are many historical doors from around the world. Some of these doors have fascinating stories passed from generation to generation, and others have a religious, cultural and political impact on society.

1. The Number 10

The Number 10 door is located at 10 Downing Street in the City of Westminster. This is the headquarters of the executive branch of the British Government, and also where the Prime Minister of England lives. The door is all black, has an arched glass transom with white pillars located on each side. In the top center part of the door is a white 10. The door has looked the same since 1772.

2. The Columbus Door

The bronze Columbus Doors were made in Germany in 1855. They feature nine panels depicting Christopher Columbus' life from 1487 til 1506. The first panel of the nine is an image of Columbus before the Council of Salamanca. He was trying to convince King Ferdinand of his new route to India. The last panel display Columbus on his deathbed. Columbus landing in the New World is shown at the very top of the transom. The doors are now featured as the entrance to the Rotunda, which is in the center of the U.S. Capitol Building.

3. Florence Baptistery Doors

The Florence Baptistery Doors are also known as the Baptistery of Saint John. Baptistery of Saint John is the oldest buildings in Florence, Italy constructed between 1059 and 1128. It is well known for the large bronze doors that were deemed by artist Michelangelo as the Gates of Paradise. It has a total of 28 panels on the door. The top 20 panels depicted the life of St. John the Baptist while the lower eight represent the eight virtues.

Oh Yes! What are they? The Virtues . . . Let name them.

1. __Hope_____
2. __F_____
3. __C_____
4. __Humility_____
5. __F_____
6. __T_____
7. __J_____
8. __P_____

Answer in back of book

4. All Saints Church: The 95 Theses

The doorway to the All Saints Church in Wittenberg, Germany wouldn't be famous if it weren't for the actions of Martin Luther. On Oct 31, 1517, he wrote <u>the 95 theses</u>. The <u>95 theses</u> were a list of grievances against the Catholic Church. Martin Luther then nailed the list to the door of the All Saints Church. This sparked the Protestant Reformation. In 1760, the All Saints Church was destroyed in a fire during the Seven Years' War. The church was later rebuilt and in 1858, a commemorative bronze door was built in the location of the original door.

5. Entryway to the Westminster Abbey

It was discovered in 2005 that the oak doors of the Westminster Abbey were installed in the 1050's. This makes them the only surviving Anglo-Saxon doors in Britain. The Westminster Abbey was formally known as the Collegiate Church of St. Peter at Westminster. It is one of the most well-known religious buildings in the United Kingdom. There have been 16 royal weddings since 1100.

6. Holy Door of St. Peter's Basilica

One of the largest churches on earth is St. Peter's Basilica. It's also one of holiest places in the Catholic faith. The doors were designed by Michelangelo and Bramante. This church is the resting place of Saint Peter. The northernmost entrance is known as the Holy Door. This door is only opened on Holy Years by the Pope and occurs every 25 years. This represents the passing from this life into the presence of God. The next time this door will be open is 2025.

7. The Palmer House Hotel in Chicago

The original Palmer House opened on September 26, 1871. It was built as a wedding gift for Potter Palmer to his bride Bertha Honore, and 13 days later, it burned down during the Great Chicago Fire. The Palmer House was rebuilt and considered one of the world's fanciest hotels. In 1920, downtown Chicago decided to add 25 more stories to the hotel. The Palmer House was purchased by Conrad Hilton December of 1945 and thereafter known as the Palmer House Hilton. On the Monroe Street side of the building, there are two large bronze doors with peacocks on them. They were specially designed by Louis Comfort Tiffany, been the same doors since 1873 reopening.

8. The Ishtar Gate

The Ishtar Gate was built around 575 B.C. by order of King Nebuchadnezzar II. It is the eighth gate to the inner city of Babylon the north side of the city. It was dedicated to Ishtar who is the goddess of fertility, love, war and sex. The gate is a deep blue covered in lapis lazuli stone with cedar roof and doors. On the door is an inscription of the dragon God Marduk surrounded by golden lions and bulls. In the early 20th century the door was excavated and reconstructed using its original bricks. The Ishtar Gate is now found in the Pergamon Museum in Berlin.

CHAPTER 4

Discerning an Open Door

The "Word of God" gives fundamental principles to help us discern if an "open door" is really from God. The words "open door" written together occurs only once in the King James Bible, Revelation 3.

I know thy works:
behold, I have set before thee an open door,
and no man can shut it:
for thou hast a little strength,
and hast kept my word, and hast
not denied my name.
Revelation 3:8 KJV

However, several verses make reference to an "open door" in the Bible. Acts 14:27 makes reference to a door being opened. The sepulchre door is an open door, Matthew 27:60; Jesus' salvation is an open door, John 10:1- 9; The will of God is another open door, 1 Corinthians 16:9.

Upon arriving in Antioch,
they called the church together
and reported everything God
had done through them

**and how he had opened the door
of faith to the Gentiles, too.**
Acts 14:27 NLT

An "open door" is considered by many an opportunity for something bigger, better or greater. In Scripture an "open door" is often used to express the opportunity to do God's will, spread the Gospel and advance in serving Him, Acts 14:27, 2 Corinthians, 2:12, Colossians 4:3.

**Now when I went to Troas
to preach the gospel of Christ
and found the Lord had opened a door for me.**
2 Corinthians 2:12 NIV

Note of Interest: To dream of a "door" represents new opportunities and changes. To dream of an "open door" represent new opportunities, possibilities or options ready and waiting for you.

~~~

The door that God opens will not contradict His word; the Scripture. It will never go against or say the opposite of what the Bible say. If we have to compromise God's word, or we have to stretch the truth or bend Scripture to justify our "open door" then it's likely not a door that God is opening for us. Anything that contradicts his Word is a temptation, rather than an open door from God. And God's word clearly says that God does not tempt us, James 1:13-14.

**When tempted, no one should say,
"God is tempting me."
For God cannot be tempted by evil,
nor does he tempt anyone;
but each person is tempted
when they are dragged away by their
own evil desire and enticed.**
James 1:13-14 NIV

The Bible reveals that God can open doors by his providence, Acts 14:27, 2 Corinthians 2:12, Revelation 3:7-8.

**To the angel of the church in Philadelphia write:
These are words of him who is holy and
true, who holds the key of David.
What he opens no one can shut,
and what he shuts no one can open.**
Revelation 3:7 NIV

The door that God opens will be accompanied by confirmation. God often confirms a matter by two or three witnesses, Matthew 18:16. It can come from the advice of a pastor, the words of a mature saint, a person who is grounded in the Lord, prophet, evangelist or the word of God. Along with prayer, fasting, and seeking godly counsel, you should be able to tell if that "open door" is truly coming from God.

Be careful for nothing;
but in every thing by prayer and supplication
with thanksgiving let your requests
be made known unto God.
Philippians 4:6 KJV

An "open door" is an opportunity to serve God. The door that God opens will require you to lean and depend on Him. Most of the time an "open door" from God is one that will stretch and strengthen our faith. God's objective for us is to grow in faith.

For I the Lord thy God will hold thy right hand,
Saying unto thee, Fear not; I will help thee.
Isaiah 41:13 KJV

Boldly come to the throne of grace and ask God's for confirmation. God's word and godly counsel from others will help assure you that you aren't just choosing a door at random, but you've carefully walking through the one He wants you to enter.

Let us therefore come boldly
unto the throne of grace,
that we may obtain mercy,
and find grace to help in time of need.
Hebrew 4:16 KJV

I feel the unction to pray: Father, open doors of opportunity for us, so that the gospel may be proclaimed and sinners may be saved. Father God gives us strength, perseverance, and the faith to enter them. We give You all the glory, and honor in Jesus' Name. Amen.

CHAPTER 5

Opening a Spiritual Door

The two words "spiritual door" is not written in the Bible together, like "the door," "tent door," "a door," "tabernacle door," and "open door." The word "spiritual" relates to the human spirit and affects the human soul. It involves religion, religious beliefs, and God. The word "door" is explained in chapter 2. Nevertheless, a door is normally used as an opening or closing to an entranceway. So a "spiritual door" could be considered a door that is open by God which blesses us and affects our body, heart, soul, spirit and mind in a godly way.

Prayer is the first component that help opens a "spiritual door." Focus on spending quality time alone with the Lord. Your quality time with the Lord will consist of prayer along with establishing and magnifying His authority in your life. Quality time also includes spending time in God's word. It could be by reading it, meditating on it, studying it or memorizing it.

Fasting is the second component. The Bible describes four types of fasting; a regular fast, a partial fast, a full fast and a sexual fast. When prayer and fasting are combined, you are preparing the way for God to open a door in your life.

Note of Interest: <u>A regular fast</u> means refraining from eating all food but still drinks water. Matthew 4:1-2 states that after Jesus had finished fasting in the desert for forty days and forty nights, he was hungry. This verse does not say anything about Jesus being thirsty. A partial fast refers to omitting a particular meal from your diet or refraining from certain types of foods. Daniel 10:2-3 records, Daniel for three weeks ate no choice food, or meat or wine. Then in Daniel 1:12, Daniel for ten days restricted his diet to vegetables and water. A full fast is when there is no food and no water consumed. Acts 9:9 described when Paul went on a full fast for three days following his encounter with Jesus on the road to Damascus. Esther made a request for a full fast to Mordecai and the Jews who are in Susa, Esther 4:15-16. A sexual fast is recorded in 1 Corinthians 7:3-6. It states do not deprive each other except by mutual consent and for a time, so that you may devote yourselves to prayer. Then come together again so that Satan will not tempt you because of your lack of self-control.

~~~

Separation is truly necessary and is considered the third component. When you separate yourself to God, you consecrate yourself to His will. You will surrender your ways for His ways, your plans for His plans, and your thoughts for His thoughts.

For your thoughts are not your thoughts,
neither are your ways my ways,
declares the LORD.
Isaiah 55:8 NIV

Barnabas and Saul were separated by God for the work He had for them to do, Acts 13.

> **As they ministered to the Lord, and fasted,**
> **the Holy Ghost said,**
> **Separate me Barnabas and Saul for the**
> **work whereunto I have called them.**
> Acts 13:2 KJV

God separated and called the Levites in Numbers 8. Paul was separated for his work in Galatians 1.

> **Thus shalt thou separate the Levites**
> **from among the children of Israel:**
> **and the Levites shall be mine.**
> Numbers 8:14 KJV

> **But when it pleased God,**
> **who separated me from my mother's womb,**
> **and called me by his grace,**
> **To reveal his Son in me, that I might**
> **preach him among the heathen;**
> **immediately I conferred not with flesh and blood:**
> Galatians 1:15-16 KJV

When opening a "spiritual door" some of the followings may be necessary, happen or occur. Even though the door is open by the Lord, it doesn't necessary means it will be pleasant throughout the entire journey or season of the open door. Read, the words that Jesus spoke to his disciples.

I have told you these things,
so that in me you may have peace.
In this world you will have trouble.
But take heart! I have overcome the world.
John 16:33 NIV

Brief details of what may be necessary, happen or occur when a "spiritual door" is open are listed below.

1. Impartation:
The laying on of hands is believed to impart the anointing. In Acts 13, Paul and Barnabas were sent out.

"And when they had fasted and prayed,
and laid their hands on them,
they sent them away."
Acts 13:3 KJV

In the above verse, the laying on of hands happens before Barnabas and Paul's missionary journeys. It represented the official recognition of the call. The leaders of the early churches imparted their blessing and anointing by laying hands on them. There is a big difference between being sent to do a work, and just going to do a work.

2. Confrontation:

Confrontation of the enemy is necessary, sometimes. As Paul and Barnabas began their work, they were immediately confronted by demonic spirits which tried to hinder the Word of God, Acts 13. Paul immediately recognized the spirits that were at work in this person. They were the spirit of deceit, trickery, fraud, enemy of righteousness and perverting the true ways of the Lord, Acts 13:10. Paul boldly in the name of the Lord confronted them and demonstrated the power of the Holy Spirit in action, Acts 13:11. The enemy was struck blind, as a result, the governor believed the doctrine of the Lord, Acts 13:11-12.

3. Proclamation:

Apostle Paul spoke the "Word of God" to his believers and the listeners, throughout Acts 13. The "Word of God" was always spoken by Paul to anyone and everyone. Apostle Paul knew the power was in the "Word of God" and did not fail to use it. Paul's bold proclamation affected the entire city, and many were saved.

Then Paul stood up, and beckoning
with his hand said,
Men of Israel, and ye that fear God, give audience.
Acts 13:16 KJV

4. Opposition:

The Jewish leaders of the city became jealous of Paul and Barnabas influence. They began speaking against Paul and Barnabas and even expelled them from their city.

**But when the Jews saw the multitudes,
they were filled with envy,
and spake against those things
which were spoken by Paul,
contradicting and blaspheming.**
Acts 13:45 KJV

When Paul and Barnabas were persecuted, they didn't waste their time trying to defend themselves or retaliate. They quickly shook the dust off their feet and were even "filled with joy and the Holy Ghost, Acts 13:51-52. Opening a "spiritual door" in the kingdom of God will bring considerable opposition.

5. Counsel, Consolidation, Consolation

Paul never abandoned those he introduced to Christ. He planted numerous churches. He encouraged them, exhorted them, shared the Word, and helped them set up church government, Acts 14:21-24.

Scholars say Apostle Paul only started 14 churches in his lifetime. The main churches founded by Paul are the church in Corinth and Antioch. Others think there are more, for example, a church was probably established in Athens because households began to follow Christ there.

In Philippi, there were two households that surrendered to the gospel of Jesus Christ. They were Lydia and the jailer so there could be two more churches established, and the list goes on.

CHAPTER 6

Old Testament – Door(s)

The "Word of God" speaks of doors in unique and profound ways. The word "door(s)" are mention approximately 203 times in the Old Testament. It begins at Genesis 4:7, and end at Malachi 1:10. Even though the word is mentioned approximately 203 times in the Old Testament, it is not mentioned in the book of Ruth, Ezra, Lamentation, Daniel, Obadiah, Jonah, Nahum, Habakkuk, Zephaniah or Haggai. Listed below are some verses concerning the word door(s) in the Old Testament.

Verse: Genesis 4:7   NIV

If you do what is right, will you not be accepted? But if you do not do what is right, sin is crouching at your door; it desires to have you, but you must rule over it.

In this verse, God questioned Cain about his anger and attitude. Cain angry disposition moved him to the action of killing his brother, Abel.

Question: Who did Eve say God gave her to replace Abel with? _____

Verse: 2 Kings 4:4   NIV

Then go inside and shut the door behind you and your sons. Pour oil into all the jars, and as each is filled, put it to one side.

This verse is about Elisha's miracle concerning a widow's oil increase. Elisha was the chief prophet in the northern kingdom of Israel. He faithfully continues to work for the Lord as Elijah had done. In a small town, a poor widow approached Elisha. Her husband, a prophet died and left debts that she and her two sons couldn't pay. The creditor wanted to take her two sons and make them slaves for payment of the debt. She had only a small amount of oil in her home. The widow begged the Prophet Elisha for help, and the Lord miraculously provided her with enough oil to sell and pay off the debt. The above verse is part of the instructions Elisha gave the widow.

Question: What type of oil did the widow have? _____

Verse: 2 Chronicles 28:24   NIV

Ahaz gathered together the furnishings from the temple of God and cut them in pieces. He shut the doors of the Lord's temple and set up altars at every street corner in Jerusalem.

Ahaz was the king of Judah and was 20 years old when he assumed the throne of Judah and reigned for 16 years. He suspended the temple-worship, the lamps were put out, and the doors were shut to prevent the priests from entering. The people could not worship there, but on high places he made.

Question: Who was Ahaz's father? _____
_____

Verse: 2 Chronicles 29:3   NIV

In the first month of the first year of his reign, he opened the doors of the temple of the Lord and repaired them.

This verse refers to Hezekiah, who became king when he was twenty-five years old. Even though King Ahaz had closed the temple doors and set up places of idol worship throughout Jerusalem and Judah, he had a godly son, named Hezekiah, 2 Chronicles 28:24. He was a very devoted, devout man. When he became king, he immediately set out to undo the wrongs of his father. He immediate repaired and opened the doors of the temple.

*Question: How many additional years did God grant Hezekiah to live?*_____

Verse: Nehemiah 3:1   NIV

Eliashib the high priest and his fellow priests went to work and rebuilt the Sheep Gate. They dedicated it and set its doors in place, building as far as the Tower of the Hundred, which they dedicated, and as far as the Tower of Hananel.

Jerusalem's wall was destroyed by the Babylonian army around 526 BC, Jeremiah 52:12-16. The above verse refers to the rebuilding of Jerusalem's wall around 456 BC, under the leadership of Nehemiah. It took 52 days to complete the reconstruction of Jerusalem's wall. The first gate mentioned in the rebuilding of Jerusalem was known as the Sheep Gate located on the eastern wall, near the pool of Bethesda. The sheep gate was a gate through which sheep were led to the Temple for sacrifice.

Question: How many gates are there? _____

Verse: Psalm 24:7   KJV

Lift up your heads, O ye gates; and be ye lifted up, ye everlasting doors; and the King of glory shall come in.

Psalm 24 is written by David and consists of 10 verses. It's believed that David wrote Psalm 24 when the Ark of the Covenant enters the city of Jerusalem for the first time. The Ark of the Covenant is described as a gold-covered wooden chest which contained the Ten Commandments written on two stone tablets, Aaron's rod, and a pot of manna. A few years earlier the elders of Israel decided to take the Ark out on the battlefield against the Philistine. Israel was defeated at the battle of Eben-Ezer, and the Ark was captured by the Philistines. After the Ark was among them for seven months, they had nothing but misfortune. The Philistines on the advice of their diviners returned the Ark to the Israelites, along with offerings. In Psalm 24, twice David speaks of lifting up the gates and doors, presumably the gates and doors of the city, so that the King of Glory might enter, referring to the Ark of the Covenant entering the city.

Question: What are the measurements of the Ark? _____

Verse: Psalm 141:3   NIV

Set a guard over my mouth, LORD; keep watch over the door of my lips.

Psalm 141 is a prayer written by David. It's a plea to God for protection from our enemies and the temptation to sin. In the time of persecution by men we are liable to speak hastily. David asks God to help him in keeping the door of his lips close, except when something good and true is to be said.

Question: What Psalm does David describes the Lord as his shepherd?_____

Verse: Proverbs 8:34   KJV

Blessed is the man that heareth me, watching daily at my gates, waiting at the post of my doors.

Solomon, the son of King David, spoke 3,000 proverbs, 1 Kings 4:32. The book of Proverbs contains some of them. Proverbs 8 shows the characteristic of a Christian. They hear, watch and wait at the post of Christ's doors.

Question: Jesus also spoke of "blessed are" known as The Beautitudes, Matthew 5:1–12. Name Just One, there are 8 to choose from . . . smile_____

Verse: Hosea 2:15   NIV

There I will give her back her vineyards, and make the Valley of Achor a door of hope. There she will respond as in the days of her youth, as in the day she came up out of Egypt.

The Valley of Achor name comes from Achan. He was an Israelite who fought at the battle of Jericho with Joshua. God had commanded them to destroy the entire city because of its great sin. Achan stole silver, a robe, and gold, and then hid them in his tent. His actions caused him and his family to be stoned and burned by Israel, Joshua 7:24-26. The Valley of Achor name means valley of trouble.

Question: Who life was spared at the battle of Jericho? _____

The answers to these questions are in the back of book . . .

CHAPTER 7

Gospels' Doors

The word "door" appears 19 times in the four gospel books of the King James Bible, and twice in two of those verses. The word "door" that ends with the letter "s" is mentioned only 4 times. They are all listed below with a title. Read over them several times, and try to relate the title and verse with the biblical event they surround. It really blessed me. Be blessed.

First, let's name the four Gospels of the Bible?

1._____
2._____
3._____
4._____

Answer in back of book

Note of Interest: The word "Gospel" is derived from two Anglo-Saxon words, the "God," meaning "good," and "spell" meaning "tidings" or "history." The four writers of the Gospels are called "Evangelists" which mean "bringer of good tidings." The Gospels give the good news concerning Jesus, the Son of God. The first three Gospels (Matthew, Mark, Luke) are called Synoptic Gospels because they give a synopsis of Christ's life. The word "synopsis" is a Greek word which means "view together." So these Gospels may be viewed together. The Synoptic Gospels are striking in their similarities. They narrate Christ's ministry chiefly in Galilee which includes His miracles, parables, and addresses to the multitudes. John's gospel portrays Jesus as the Son of God.

~~~

Praying Behind A Closed Door   Matthew 6:6 KJV

But thou, when thou prayest, enter into thy closet, and when thou hast shut thy door, pay to thy Father which is in secret; and thy Father which seeth in secret shall reward thee openly.

The Coming of the Son of Man   Matthew 24:33 KJV

So likewise ye, when ye shall see all these things, know that it is near, even at the doors.

The Parable of the Ten Virgins   Matthew 25:10 NLT

But while they were gone to buy oil, the bridegroom came. Then those who were ready went in with him to the marriage feast, and the door was locked.

The Burial of Jesus   Matthew 27:60 KJV

And laid it in his own new tomb, which he had hewn out in the rock: and he rolled a great stone to the door of the sepulchre, and departed.

The Resurrection   Matthew 28:2 KJV

And, behold, there was a great earthquake: for the angel of the Lord descended from heaven, and came and rolled back the stone from the door, and sat upon it.

Jesus Heals Many People   Mark 1:33 NLT

The whole town gathered at the door to watch.

Jesus Heals a Paralyzed Man   Mark 2:2 NLT

Soon the house where he was staying was so packed with visitors that there was no more room, even outside the door. While he was preaching God's word to them.

Jesus' Triumphant Entry   Mark 11:4 NLT

The two disciples left and found the colt standing in the street, tied outside the front door.

Signs of the End Times   Mark 13:29 NIV

Even so, when you see these things happening, you know that it is near, right at the door.

The Burial of Jesus   Mark 15:46 KJV

And he brought fine linen, and took him down, and wrapped him in the linen, and laid him in a sepulchre which was hewn out of a rock, and rolled a stone unto the door of the sepulchre.

Jesus Has Risen   Mark 16:3 KJV

And they said among themselves, Who shall roll us away the stone from the door of the sepulchre?

Teaching about Prayer   Luke 11:7 KJV

And he from within shall answer and say, Trouble me not: the door is now shut, and my children are with me in bed; I cannot rise and give thee.

The Narrow Door   Luke 13:24-25 NIV

Make every effort to enter through the narrow door, because many, I tell you, will try to enter and will not be able to. Once the owner of the house gets up and closes the door, you will stand outside knocking and pleading, "Sir, open the door for us.

The Good Shepherd and His Sheep   John 10:1- 2 KJV

Verily, verily, I say unto you, He that entereth not by the door into the sheepfold, but climbeth up some other way, the same is a thief and a robber. But he that entered in by the door is the shepherd of the sheep.

I Am   John 10:7 KJV

Then said Jesus unto them again, Verily, verily, I say unto you, I am the door of the sheep.

The Door   John 10:9 KJV

I am the door: by me if any man enter in, he shall be shave, and shall go in and out, and find pasture.

Peter's First Denial   John 18:16 NIV

But Peter had to wait outside at the door. The other disciple, who was known to the high priest, came back, spoke to the servant girl on duty there and brought Peter in.

Damsel at the Door   John 18:17 KJV

Then saith the damsel that kept the door unto Peter, Art not thou also one of this man's disciples? He saith, I am not.

Jesus Appears to His Disciples   John 20:19 NIV

On the evening of that first day of the week, when the disciples were together, with the doors locked for fear of the Jewish leaders, Jesus came and stood among them and said, "Peace be with you!"

Jesus Appears to Thomas   John 20:26 KJV

And after eight days again his disciples were within, and Thomas with them: then came Jesus, the doors being shut, and stood in the midst, and said, Peace be unto you.

CHAPTER 8

Twelve Times

The word "door" is mention twelve times in the New Testament (KJV); not including the Gospels of Jesus Christ. The word "door" is mentioned five times in the book of Acts, which is also called the Acts of the Apostles. It is mentioned only once in 1 Corinthians, 2 Corinthians, Colossians and James. The word "door" is mentioned three times in Revelation. All twelve verses are listed below with several I chose to briefly discuss.

Ananias and Sapphira

Acts 5:9   KJV

Then Peter said unto her, How is it that ye have agreed together to tempt the Spirit of the Lord? Behold, the feet of them which have buried thy husband are at the door, and shall carry thee out.

Luke wrote this biblical event 40 days after Jesus rose from the grave. A married couple named Ananias and Sapphira both lied to the Apostles. The people in the region were selling their property and bringing the money from the sale to the Apostles. The money given to the Apostles were used to help the poor and needy. Ananias and Sapphira decided they would not give all the money to the Apostle, but keep part of it, and lied about it. Ananias lied first to the Apostles and fell dead.

About three hours later, Sapphira came to the Apostles, not knowing what had happened to her husband, lied and then fell dead, too. She was taken away and buried beside her husband.

Peter's Miraculous Escape
Acts 12:6   KJV
And when Herod would have brought him forth, the same night Peter was sleeping between two soldiers, bound with two chains: and the keepers before the door kept the prison.

Peter Knocked at the Door
Acts 12:13   KJV
And as Peter knocked at the door of the gate, a damsel came to hearken, named Rhoda.

Peter Continued Knocking
Acts 12:16   KJV
But Peter continued knocking: and when they had opened the door, and saw him, they were astonished.

Acts 12:6, 13 and 16 surround Peter's third imprisonment, and his miraculous prison escape. The believers were gathered in prayer at the home of Mary. This Mary is the aunt of Barnabas and the mother of Mark. They had been praying for Peter day and night because he was in prison. Herod had thrown Peter in prison, and he was guarded by a squad of four soldiers. Peter was sleeping peacefully chained between two soldiers when an angel awakens him. The angel tells him to get up, quickly. The chains which kept Peter bounded to the soldiers fall off his hands. The angel told Peter to get dressed and put on his sandals. The angel led Peter by two more guards and then to the prison gate. As the two walked down the street, the angel left Peter. Peter went to the house where he knew the believers were gathered and knocked on the door. Rhoda, a servant girl came to the door. As soon as she heard Peter's voice she was so excited she ran back into the house without letting Peter in. She shouted, "Peter is at the door!" The believers told her, "She was out of her mind." It's not mentioned how long it took Rhoda to convince the believers that Peter was at the door. Meanwhile, Peter continues to knock on the door.

Open Door of Faith to the Gentiles
Acts 14:27   KJV

And when they were come, and had gathered the church together, they rehearsed all that God had done with them, and how he had opened the door of faith unto the Gentiles.

A Great Door
1 Corinthians 16:9   KJV

For a great door and effectual is opened unto me, and there are many adversaries.

The Door of Preaching
2 Corinthians 2:12   KJV

Furthermore, when I came to Troas to preach Christ's gospel, and a door was opened unto me of the Lord.

The Door of Utterance

Colossians 4:3   KJV

Withal praying also for us, that God would open unto us a door of utterance, to speak the mystery of Christ, for which I am also in bonds.

Paul had suffered under Jewish malice and was thrown in prison for preaching the Gospel. Paul reminds the believers to be devoted to prayer, and pray that the message of Christ is presented everywhere. The phrase "door of utterance" signifies an occasion, opportunity or an open door for the doctrine of the Gospel to be spoken.

Exhortation by James

James 5:9   KJV

Grudge not one against another, brethren, lest ye be condemned: behold, the judge standeth before the door.

James, the half-brother of the Lord, wrote to the twelve tribes that were scattered throughout the surrounding regions of the Roman Empire. They were facing persecution against the Jewish leaders is what cause them to flee their cities and towns. This letter was written to encourage them to practice patient among each other, reminds them not to be grumblers and complainers in their hardship, and continue to show love for each other because the Judge stands at the door.

A Door No Man can Shut

Revelation 3:8   KJV

I know thy works: behold, I have set before thee an open door, and no man can shut it: for thou hast a little strength, and hast kept my word, and hast not denied my name.

This verse was written to the church in Philadelphia by John while he was on the island of Patmos. This verse indicates they lack spiritual strength, but it doesn't stop them from keeping God's word or denying His name. This verse also shows that they have one excellent quality which is faithfulness. Christ opens the door to the Kingdom because of the Philadelphians' faithfulness.

Note of Interest: Out of the seven churches, only Smyrna and Philadelphia receive special praise from the Lord.

A Door of Salvation
Revelation 3:20   KJV

Behold, I stand at the door, and knock: if any man hear my voice, and open the door, I will come in to him, and will sup with him, and he with me.

An Open Heavenly Door
Revelation 4:1   KJV

After this I looked, and behold, a door was opened in heaven: and the first voice which I heard was as it were of a trumpet talking with me; which said, Come up hither, and I will shew thee things which must be hereafter.

This is the first of a series of visions which John had on the Greek island of Patmos. He was banished there because he wouldn't stop preaching the Gospel. According to tradition, he was sentenced to death by being thrown into a cauldron of boiling oil. When that didn't harm him, he was sent to Patmos. While there he was visited by the Lord who commanded him to write what he sees in the visions.

The Book of Acts also contains five verses that speak on "doors." They are listed below with a brief introductory title.

1.	Angel Open the Doors	Acts 5:9	KJV
2.	Standing Before the Doors	Acts 5:23	KJV
3.	All Doors were Opened	Acts 16:26	KJV
4.	The Prison Doors	Acts 16:27	KJV
5.	Temple Doors Shut	Acts 21:30	KJV

QUESTION AND ANSWER

This new section, just dropped in my spirit at 0613 on January 14, 2017, titled A Reader's Question.

An individual asked me what I meant by the statement below. Eventhough, it been over a year or so, I woke up this morning with that question on my mind. I prayed about it, got up from my knees, fix me some coffee and to started to reading over this book, once again. When I got to Author's Notes and read over that statement, the Holy Spirit in a sweet, still unction said, "Answer that Question."

The statement:
The times and dates of researching, reading, and gathering this information are not included; mostly when I typed on it.

In essence, this is how I answered that question:

There are times that I may copy certain pages from the different Bible translations and read over them in bed, many, many, many, many, many, many times.

There are times that I may print numerous informative materials off the internet and read over them for days at home, on my lunch break, in the park, at the beauty shop, sitting on the front porch or by a waterfront.

There are times I may reread old books in my bookcase, read over my old notes from Bible classes and Seminary studies.

Then the majority of the time, I would pray about what I have read, fast and seek God's face. Basically, asking Father God what to, where to and how to place what I have pondered and meditated on in His book. Those times and dates are not written in the book; they are what I refer to as researching, reading and gathering information.

Praying that this answer will encourage and be a blessing to others, too.

Author's Closing Remarks

God can make a way out of no way, open doors that no man can close and close doors no man can open. When God opens a door, He also gives us strength to go through it. He will never leave us, forsake us or place on us more than we can bear. When Father God closes a door, we shouldn't try to force our way through it. He knows what is best for us.

When one door closes, another one opens,
but we often look so long and so
regretfully upon the closed door
that we do not see the one that has opened for us.
Alexander Graham Bell

As We wrap up our Ministry with You,
Pray for the Ministry . . .

May the "LORD of Peace," Himself give you His Peace in every circumstance and at every door that you face on your pilgrimage journey.

Dr. Vanessa

References

Chapter 1
1. Wikipedia, The Free Encyclopedia:
    https://wikipedia.org/wiki/Book_of_Revelation
2. Wikipedia, The Free Encyclopedia:
    https://wikipedia.org/wiki/
    Regligion_in_the_Middle_East

Chapter 2
1. Dictionary: https://dictionary.com/browse/door
2. Wikipedia, The Free Encyclopedia: https://wikipedia.
    org/wiki/Door

Chapter 3
1. 10 World Famous Doors: https://improvement.
    com/a/10-world-famous-doors,
2. Wikipedia, The Free Encyclopedia: https://wikipedia.
    org/wikie/Ishtar_Gate

Chapter 4
1. BibleGateway: https://www.biblegateway.com

Chapter 5
1. BibleGateway: https://biblegateway.com
2. Wikipedia, The Free Encyclopedia:
    https://en.wikipedia.org/wiki/fasting

Chapter 6
1. BibleGateway: https://www.biblegateway.com
2. Wikipedia, The Free Encyclopedia:
    https://en.wikipedia.org/wiki/Elisha
3. Wikipedia, The Free Encyclopedia:
    https://en.wikipedia.org/wiki/Ahaz

Chapter 7
1. BibleGateway: https://www.biblegateway.com
2. Jacksonville Theological Seminary: Harmony of the
    Gospel Class Notes, 10/2006

Chapter 8
1. BibleGateway: https://www.biblegateway.com

Answers & Information Section

Chapter 1

The Apostle John was given messages to the seven churches in Asia which are listed below.

1. Ephesus
Didn't lose love for God's truth or His people, Revelation 2:1-7

2. Smyrna
Remain faithful in the face of tribulation and poverty, Revelation 2:8-11

3. Pergamos
Resist Satan's influence event to death, if necessary, Revelation 2:12-17

4. Thyatira
Resist false teaching, Revelation 2:18-29

5. Sardis
Remain zealous and pure in conduct, Revelation 3:1-6

6. Philadelphia
Persevere and walk through the doors God opens, Revelation 3:10

7. Laodicea

Don't become lukewarm about God's way of life, Revelation 14:22

Chapter 2

The eight virtues are:

1. Hope
2. Faith
3. Charity
4. Humility
5. Fortitude
6. Temperance
7. Justice
8. Prudence

Chapter 6

1. *Who did Eve say God gave her to replace Abel with?* Seth
2. *What type of oil did the widow have?* Olive
3. *Who was Ahaz's father?* Jotham
4. *How many additional years did God grant Hezekiah to live?*

    God granted Hezekiah 15 more years, this shows God's mercy and that He listened to prayers of the obedient.

5. *How many gates are there?*

    There are 12 gates and they are listed below.

    1. The Valley Gate
    2. The Gate of the Fountain

3. The Sheep Gate
4. The Fish Gate
5. The Old Gate
6. The Dung Gate
7. The Water Gate
8. The Horse Gate
9. The East Gate
10. The Gate of Miphkad
11. The Gate of Ephraim
12. The Prison Gate

6. *What are the measurements of the Ark?*
    The Ark was a 2 ½ x 1 ½ cubit (45 x 27 inches; 3.75 ft. x 2.25 ft.) rectangular wooden chest with its lid being the Mercy seat with the Cherubim of glory facing each other with wings outstretched.

7. *What Psalm does David describes the Lord as his shepherd?*
    Psalm 23

8. *Jesus also spoke of "blessed are" known as The Beautitudes, Matthew 5:1-12. Name Just One, there are 8 to choice from . . .*
    smile

    1. Blessed are the poor in spirit, for theirs is the kingdom of heaven.
    2. Blessed are they who mourn, for they shall be comforted.
    3. Blessed are the meek, for they shall inherit the earth.
    4. Blessed are they who hunger and thirst for righteousness, for they shall be satisfied.

5. Blessed are the merciful, for they shall obtain mercy.
6. Blessed are the pure in heart, for they shall see God.
7. Blessed are the peacemakers, for they shall be called children of God.
8. Blessed are they who are persecuted for the sake of righteousness, for theirs is the kingdom of heaven.

9. Who life was spared at the battle of Jericho?

Rahab, the prostitute and her family lives were spared.

Chapter 7

The four Gospels Books of the Bible are Matthew, Mark, Luke & John. A gospel is an account describing the life, death, and resurrection of Jesus of Nazareth.

OTHER BOOKS BY THE AUTHOR

From the Pew to the Pulpit   Published: 08/29/2007

Isaiah 26:3-4 "Perfect Peace"   Published: 09/07/2010

Isaiah 26:3-4 "Perfect Peace"   Published: 02/13/2012
The Last Single Digit

Isaiah 26:3-4 "Perfect Peace   Published: 10/24/2012
III" Silver and Gold

Isaiah 26:3-4 "Perfect Peace   Published: 04/10/2013
IV" The Kingdom Number

Isaiah 26:3-4 "Perfect Peace V" Published: 09/06/2013
2541

Isaiah 26:3-4 "Perfect Peace   Published: 02/28/2014
VI" Zacchaeus

Isaiah 26:3-4 "Perfect Peace   Published: 10/29/2014
VII" Eleven

Isaiah 26:3-4 "Perfect Peace   Published: 05/22/2015
VIII" Prayer

Isaiah 26:3-4 "Perfect Peace   Published: 10/26/2015
IX" Sixteen

Isaiah 26:3-4 "Perfect Peace X" Published: 04/12/2016
Dreams

Printed in the United States
By Bookmasters